Down the Dart

Boat trip from Totnes to Dartmouth

Chips Barber

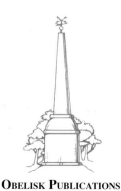

OBELISK PUBLICATIONS

ALSO BY THE AUTHOR:

Ten Family Bike Rides in Devon
Ten Family Walks on Dartmoor • Six Short Pub Walks on Dartmoor
Short Circular Walks in and around Sidmouth • Walks on and around Woodbury Common
Diary of a Devonshire Walker • From The Dart to The Start
The Great Little Dartmoor Book • The Great Little Exeter Book
The Great Little Totnes Book • The Great Little Plymouth Book • The Great Little Chagford Book
Made in Devon *(with David FitzGerald)* • The Lost City of Exeter – Revisited
The Dartmoor Quiz Book • Place-Names in Devon • An A to Z of Devon Dialect
Dark & Dastardly Dartmoor • The Ghosts of Exeter • Haunted Pubs in Devon
Exmouth in Colour • Plymouth in Colour • Beautiful Exeter
Colourful Dartmoor • Colourful Cockington • Topsham in Colour
The South Hams in Colour • Torbay in Colour – Torquay, Paignton, Brixham
Sidmouth Past and Present • Topsham Past and Present • Honiton Past and Present
Seaton & Axmouth • Beer • Branscombe • Colyton & Colyford
Around & About Salcombe • Around & About Lustleigh
Around & About Hope Cove and Thurlestone
Around & About Burgh Island and Bigbury-on-Sea
Around & About Tavistock • Around & About Roborough Down
Kingskerswell of Yesteryear *(with John Hand)*
Shaldon & Ringmore • Lydford & Brent Tor • Torquay • Paignton • Brixham
Devon's Amazing Men of God *(with Walter Jacobson)*
Brixham of Yesteryear, Parts I, II and III • Pinhoe of Yesteryear, Parts I and II
Princetown of Yesteryear, Parts I and II • The Teign Valley of Yesteryear, Parts I and II
Widecombe – A Visitor's Guide • Bickleigh – A Visitor's Guide
Newton Ferrers and Noss Mayo • Along The Otter • Along The Tavy • Along The Avon
Railways on and around Dartmoor • Devon's Railways of Yesteryear
Chagford of Yesteryear • Dartmoor of Yesteryear
Exminster of Yesteryear • Dartmouth of Yesteryear
Heavitree of Yesteryear • Sidmouth of Yesteryear • Whipton of Yesteryear
Plymouth Hoe • Tiverton • The Story of Dawlish Warren
The Story of Hallsands • The Story of Dartmoor Prison
Dawlish of Yesteryear • Discovering Devon…Dawlish
Walk the East Devon Coast – Lyme Regis to Lympstone
Walk the South Devon Coast – Dawlish Warren to Dartmouth
Walk the South Hams Coast – Dartmouth to Salcombe
Walk the South Hams Coast – Salcombe to Plymouth

OTHER TITLES FROM THIS AREA INCLUDE:

The Ghosts of Totnes • Buckfast and Buckfastleigh, *Bob Mann*
Villages of The South Hams, *John Legge* • The Ghosts of Brixham, *Graham Wyley*
Dart Country • A Secret Circle • The Ghosts of Berry Pomeroy Castle, *Deryck Seymour*
Around the Churches of The South Hams, Parts I and II, *Walter Jacobson*

We have many other Devon titles. For a current list, please send an SAE to
Obelisk Publications at 2 Church Hill, Pinhoe, Exeter EX4 9ER.
Or visit out website at www.ObeliskPublications.com

First published in 2004, reprinted in 2010 by
Obelisk Publications, 2 Church Hill, Pinhoe, Exeter, Devon EX4 9ER
Designed and typeset by Sally Barber
Printed in Great Britain
by Short Run Press Ltd, Exeter, Devon

Down the Dart

Boat trip from Totnes to Dartmouth

"Welcome aboard the *Titanic*," jokes the narrator, ready to entertain yet another boatload of passengers on the 75-minute river trip between Totnes and Dartmouth. Beautiful houses, local legends, household names, stories of the valley, villages and other places along the way, will all feature in the 12-mile journey between these two ancient port towns. By the time attentive and observant passengers step ashore at Dartmouth, they will be well versed in the history and geography of the river and its immediate environs.

This guide book is intended to act as a lasting keepsake for those who undertake this splendid river journey. A wide range of illustrations is included.

The old picture postcards portray river journeys of the past, whilst the more modern aerial pictures in the second half of the book reveal a different perspective of the wider valley. To give another dimension to the boat trip, many of the illustrations are views which would not be seen from the river.

But, before we set out from the Steamer Quay, what of Totnes, the place of embarkation? It is unique – there is no place quite like it! The ancient town sits at the top of the estuary, and also at the lowest bridging point on the river. One of the four ancient boroughs of Devon, trade and expansion in Totnes seemed to slow down after Elizabethan times. Since then other less exotic Devonshire places have outstripped the town in the population stakes; Totnes was a thriving town when Torquay was a humble hamlet. The town remains compact as it doesn't really lend itself to massive expansion. But size isn't everything! The late, and esteemed historian, Professor W. G. Hoskins wrote: *Totnes is, next to Exeter and Plymouth, the most interesting town in Devon, a lively little place…*

Legend has it that this was the place where Brutus of Troy, a Trojan Prince, first stepped ashore on English soil. Hard 'evidence' lies in the Brutus Stone, located in the pavement of Fore Street, below the East Gate.

Down the Dart

Brutus was searching for an island promised to him by the Goddess Diana. In 1170 BC, after the Trojan Wars, he set out on his quest. These are the words he is alleged to have uttered on arrival: *"Here I stand, and here I rest. The town shall be called Totnes."* Apparently, the name 'Britain' is thus derived from Brutus. However, in the country's capital, 'The London Stone' has a similar tale attached to it, involving the same personnel. This time the ancient proverb runs: *"So long as the stone of Brutus is safe, so long shall London flourish."* As it doesn't even rhyme, we Devonians prefer to think the greater claim is ours!

With a name meaning 'the fort on the nose of land', Totnes was established in Saxon times on a high site overlooking the Dart Valley; it was well positioned to defend itself against the marauding Vikings.

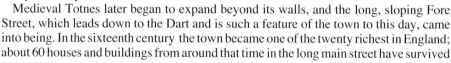

It became a market and trading centre, and even minted its own coins. After the Norman conquest, Totnes was given to a knight called Judhael, who had the Castle built. The view shown here was taken from the main road to Kingsbridge.

The castle is open to the public during the tourist season; it is managed by English Heritage, as is the nearby heavily haunted ruin of Berry Pomeroy Castle, about a mile and a half outside the town.

Medieval Totnes later began to expand beyond its walls, and the long, sloping Fore Street, which leads down to the Dart and is such a feature of the town to this day, came into being. In the sixteenth century the town became one of the twenty richest in England; about 60 houses and buildings from around that time in the long main street have survived into the present day.

If you get the opportunity, a visit to the ancient Guildhall, behind the church, is well worthwhile. It is full of interest and includes a memorial to Totnes-born William Wills (1834–1861). He was a hero in Australian exploration history for being the navigator on the first journey to be completed across the vast, parched interior of the country.

With Robert O'Hara Burke in command, he was in a small party which travelled northwards from Melbourne to reach the Gulf of Carpentaria. Tragically, owing to a breakdown in communications, both Burke and Wills perished near Cooper's Creek on the return journey. The approximate spot where Wills's body was found is marked by an old iron wagon axle and a ring of stones. Nearby, a newer cairn, complete with tablet, forms a small shrine to a major achievement. In the 1985 film portrayal of this epic story, the part of Wills was played by Nigel Havers.

Down the Dart

Closer to his home, there is also an obelisk dedicated to Wills at the entrance to The Plains, a stone's throw from Totnes Bridge.

Totnes has an exceptionally fine museum, located just below the East Gate clock. It is far bigger than its frontage may suggest, and holds many treasures of local history. Sometimes dubbed 'the Father of the Modern Computer', local man Charles Babbage (1791–1871) is well represented. In 2002, in the BBC poll to find the '100 Greatest Britons', he just missed the top 50 by one place!

If you want to know more about the town's other buildings and attractions, then please read another of my books, *The Great Little Totnes Book*. However, if it's the supernatural which takes your fancy, then Bob Mann's *The Ghosts of Totnes* is highly recommended. Such an ancient place is bound to have a strong resident population of spooks, and this town does not disappoint.

But time and tide wait for no man, and the boat is ready to transport us the 12 miles or so down river to Dartmouth. Travelling at a maximum of about 6 knots (or 7 mph), it is possible to relax and enjoy the serenity of this green, winding corridor. All along the way there are different things to see: a constantly changing scene, whatever the season.

6

Organised journeys between Totnes and Dartmouth have been enjoyed by many generations. These two photographs (the one at the bottom of page 6 in winter, the one above in summer) show the Steamer Quay at Totnes in the days when paddle steamers plied the river. Although the scene has now changed, it is still clearly recognisable. In the wintry view, the slim-line *Kingswear Castle* is moored at the quayside. This vessel will be seen later in a much sadder state of repair...

In the summer view, Totnes Bridge appears to the left. This was engineered by Charles Fowler, who also designed Covent Garden Market: another Devonshire lad made good.

Looking down on the Dart, this elevated view was taken from the Sharpham Drive, which now makes an excellent route for a walk to Ashprington. In the far distance, the outline of Dartmoor can be spied, whilst in the middle distance, the lower hills of the Dartington estate are prominent. To the left of the picture, the bold, red sandstone tower of Totnes Church rises above the town centre rooftops. The sailing ship in the centre is moored opposite Vire Island, so named in 1973 to commemorate the twinning of Totnes with this Normandy town. Prior to this it was simply 'The Island'. The Dart flows from the right of it, but its course is masked from view by the dense tree cover. Both banks of the river have witnessed immense change since this photograph was taken, particularly below Steamer Quay.

Meanwhile, back on board, having been given precise details of what to do in an emergency, our attention is soon turned to the immediate surroundings. The first impressions are not entirely favourable – on the left, modern business units seem out of keeping. In contrast, this old picture postcard shows a more rural scene, looking along this river bank in the direction of Totnes.

Heading downstream, on the right-hand side of the river, a long, narrow boatyard now occupies Baltic Wharf – so named because from 1896 Scandinavian and Russian timber was imported here, the boats coming through the Baltic on the way. The trade lasted for almost a century.

This 1980s picture looks back towards the town, with both the church tower and the castle as prominent landmarks. Inevitably, the riverside warehouses on the left have gone, to be replaced by houses and apartments.

No doubt many people will recall the sailing adventures of Pete Goss, whose ill-fated *Team Philips* catamaran was built here. He came to the attention of the general public during the 1996/7 Vendée Globe round-the-world single-handed yacht race. He bravely risked his own life during a Southern Ocean hurricane, by turning back several hundred miles to rescue Raphael Dinelli, a French sailor. By doing so, Goss also sacrificed the substantial lead that he held. For his bravery and gallantry, this hero of the high seas, and former Royal Marine, was awarded the *Légion d'honneur*.

Team Philips created huge interest and drew vast crowds of onlookers whenever the giant craft took to the water. Billed by one observer as "*Howards' Way* meets *Star Wars*" (a reference to a television series and a fantasy film), the catamaran was regularly touted as being 'bigger than the Centre Court at Wimbledon' and 'with enough room to park 80 cars between its two giant 120-ft-long hulls'. (They didn't actually do this, of course!) The massive masts towered 130 feet above water level, taller than a stack of ten double-decker buses. (Or try this either!) However, its revolutionary design led to enormous problems. It had already suffered teething troubles off the Scilly Isles; while undergoing further trials, it began to break up during a storm in the Atlantic and had to be abandoned. Thus ended Pete Goss's dream of winning 'The Race'.

Created by the Duke of Somerset in the nineteenth century, the Longmarsh runs along the eastern side of the river. Part of it used to be a rifle range, shown on the 1907 map extract. It has since been artificially raised several feet to prevent flooding.

Just to the south of this, on the other bank of Home Reach, is the quaintly named World's End. Although commonly used for pubs, this name is believed to have been given as a consequence of the awful smell from a sewage farm, which pervaded the air here.

High on a hill to the left are some ruined buildings, last used in about 1900. It was here, at the aptly named Windwhistle, that a red warning flag was flown at times of firing on the range.

The extensive reed beds to the right once supplied local thatchers.

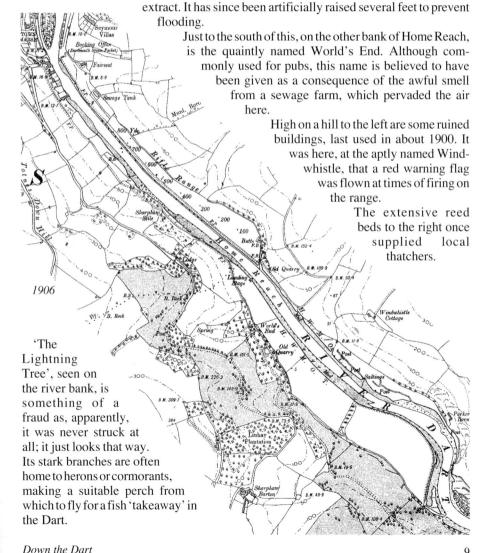

1906

'The Lightning Tree', seen on the river bank, is something of a fraud as, apparently, it was never struck at all; it just looks that way. Its stark branches are often home to herons or cormorants, making a suitable perch from which to fly for a fish 'takeaway' in the Dart.

There is an abundance of wildlife to be seen along the way, and the cruise commentator will knowledgeably point out all sorts of creatures seen on, in, and beside the river, as well as those soaring high above the dense woodlands. Here are some waterfowl practising their line dancing on the water!

Totnes disappears out of sight behind us as the first significant bend is negotiated and Fleet Mill Reach entered. To the left is the dammed entrance to the former Fleet Mill creek. Rotting in the mud are the remains of the aforementioned *Kingswear Castle*, which for a score of years, between 1904 and 1924, used to ferry people up and down the river.

In her last years she served as a hospital ship; when she was past her 'sail-by' date, she was towed here and burnt to destroy any possible lingering infections.

This noble little vessel must have been carrying the engineering equivalent of a donor card, because her engines were removed and installed in the next *Kingswear Castle*. This later namesake is based in Chatham and still plies the River Medway in Kent.

Meanwhile, on the opposite bank, or starboard side, sitting majestically high above the valley, the impressive Sharpham House comes into view. It was designed in 1770 by the master mason and monumental sculptor Sir Robert Taylor.

It has a long history and owes its origin to Captain Philemon Pownall. He financed this palatial home from his share of the spoils of a captured, treasure-laden Spanish ship.

This is the gist of a memorial to him and his wife, which is found in the parish church of St David's at nearby Ashprington: *In remembrance of JANE POWNALL, who died on the 16th October 1778, aged 33 years, and of Captain PHILEMON POWNALL, who was slain in fight on 15th June 1780, aged 45 Years. This monument was erected by the executors at the desire of their only issue JANE. Reader, if thy breath has learnt to lament departed merit, refuse not the tribute of a tear to the memory of Captain Pownall, a man brave without rashness, liberal without ostentation, honest, open and sincere. Preferring the toils and perils of the ocean when the voice of his country called for his services to a life of ease and tranquillity which his affluence would have afforded, he fell a victim in her cause.*

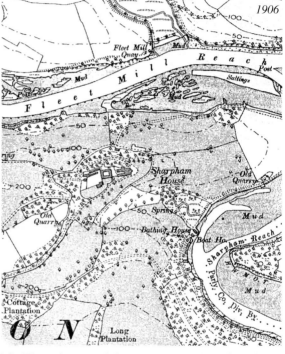

In Victorian times Richard Durant lived here; a small acknowledgement to his local influence is found in the pretty village of Ashprington, where the classy pub is called the Durant Arms. On 20 May 1856, he married Charlotte Still Dashwood, daughter of Colonel Alexander Wilton Dashwood and Marian Still. Sadly she passed away in April 1863, leaving behind Anna Marie Durant, her only child.

The Sharpham Partnership is a family business, which was established in 1981 to combine three enterprises: a dairy farm with a herd of Jersey cows; a creamery to create a range of cheeses from the milk; and a vineyard and winery.

The handsome John Henry Napper Nevill, shown here as he looked in 1906, was vicar of nearby Stoke Gabriel (1881–1916). The spinsters of the area were smitten by this tall Irishman's good looks. It has been suggested that Miss Durant, of Sharpham House, even went to the trouble of having a window specially constructed to enable her to gaze 'Nevill-wards'! He lost his status as Devon's most eligible vicar by marrying his housekeeper,

a lady who already had two children from a previous marriage. Nevill had originally intended to become a doctor, and was never shy of treating the sick, though suspicions were aroused when one of his 'patients' was buried quickly following her death. The body was exhumed, but it was discovered that she died from natural causes. As a man of the people, the vicar did his best for his parishioners. On one occasion, a well-used footpath down to the Dart was barred from use; he led a group of irate fishermen to the obstruction, produced a handsaw, and removed the problem.

The superbly located Sharpham boathouse was, in the 1970s, the home of Brian Patten, the Liverpool poet, a decade after he had established himself alongside contemporaries such as Roger McGough. His works include *Love Poems*, *Storm Damage* and *Grinning Jack*. He is also the creator of 'cult classics' for children, such as *Gargling With Jelly*, *Thawing Frozen Frogs*, *The Utter Nutters*, *Mr Moon's Last Case* and *Juggling With Gerbils*.

The River Dart at Duncannon

We navigate another chicane to pass Duncannon. This is a salmon-fishing hamlet where the cruise commentator points out the tiny fishing boats bobbing on the water. Licences are restricted, as are the traditional methods of netting the fish. Apparently the fishermen are not allowed to cast their nets on Saturdays and Sundays, so "the salmon have the weekend off"! Overlooking this delightful hamlet is Woods, a superb house built in 1897 using granite.

Little Bow Creek, the longest estuarine tributary of the Dart, and also the lowest section of the Harbourne river, lies off to the west, opposite Stoke Point. On the River Dart journey it is impossible to see as far as Tuckenhay, over a mile up river, or to see Ashprington and Cornworthy, which are high in the surrounding hills. However, if you are observant you will just spy Cornworthy's ancient church tower as you pass the entrance to Bow Creek. This is where the Revd Charles Barter gave 73 years of loyal service; he was still holding this office in 1846, the year he died at the age of 97.

Tuckenhay is a most attractive place. Its former mill made quality handmade paper used for bank notes, notably in England and America. For about six years, from 1989, Keith Floyd, the famous television chef, owned the Maltster's Arms, one of its two inns. For that brief interlude, it was called 'Floyd's Inn (Sometimes)'.

The next picture shows Tuckenhay as seen from a steep hill.

Down the Dart

I recommend a highly informative little book by John Legge entitled *Villages of the South Hams*. Three of the five settlements included are Tuckenhay, Ashprington and Cornworthy; the other two are Harbertonford and East Allington. It also contains details of the countryside between them.

The lower Dart is surrounded by many villages: soon, on the left-hand side, you will catch a glimpse of Stoke Gabriel, up another creek. This is one of the few places in Devon without street lighting; it is more or less happy to stay in the 'dark ages'.

Stoke Gabriel is an attractive village (in daylight!), and pubs such as the ancient

Church House Inn (shown here) are full of character. The ancient yew tree in the churchyard is more than a thousand years old; it has to be seen to be believed, with its heavy branches well propped up. In a survey, where some 800 ancient yew trees were examined, this one was selected as being in the top 12 of note. It is well worth visiting in its own right; if you do, just remember to duck !

Stoke Gabriel

George Jackson Churchward (1857–1933) of Stoke Gabriel was a brilliant mathematician who used this ability to great purpose. From the age of 16 he worked as a probationer engineer on the South Devon Railway in the engine sheds at Newton Abbot, but was soon transferred to Swindon, where he was to spend his working life. In 1900 he became the first mayor of this newly created borough. Educated at Totnes Grammar School, he designed some of the most famous railway locomotives of his day, including the *Saint* and *Star* express engines. It was the *City of Truro* that brought Churchward national fame in 1903, as it was the first locomotive to clock a speed in excess of 100 mph. He also designed railway carriages.

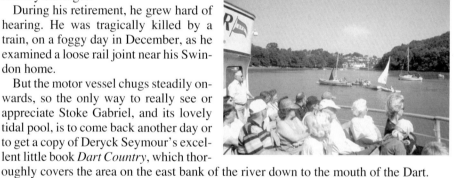

During his retirement, he grew hard of hearing. He was tragically killed by a train, on a foggy day in December, as he examined a loose rail joint near his Swindon home.

But the motor vessel chugs steadily onwards, so the only way to really see or appreciate Stoke Gabriel, and its lovely tidal pool, is to come back another day or to get a copy of Deryck Seymour's excellent little book *Dart Country*, which thoroughly covers the area on the east bank of the river down to the mouth of the Dart.

The history lesson continues, with the left bank still taking centre stage for the time being. Overlooking the river are some impressive properties. Sandridge Park, built for the widow of the second Lord Ashburton, is an imposing Italianate mansion designed in 1802 by John Nash (1752–1835), whose achievements included much of the layout of Regency London. He designed Trafalgar Square, created Buckingham Palace out of the original Buckingham House, and designed Marble Arch. For good measure, and to show his versatility, he also remodelled the Royal Pavilion at Brighton. The house is on a site

previously occupied by the Sandridges, who had first settled here in the reign of Henry II. At one time Nash was apprentice to the aforementioned Sir Robert Taylor, thereby linking two of the valley's most famous and stylish houses.

14

Sandridge Barton lies close by. It is reputed to be the birthplace of John Davis (c.1550–1605), one of the chief navigators in the reign of Queen Elizabeth I. His journeys took him to far-off lands – from the Falklands to Baffin Island, off Canada. His elusive quest was to find a North-West Passage, but his main 'function' seems to have been the pinpointing of huge amounts of fish and fur-bearing animals. Whilst in warmer waters, he met a brutal death at the hands of Japanese pirates. The 400-mile-long Davis Strait, between Greenland and Baffin Island, is named after this intellectual, whose written works on navigation set the standard for his era.

1906

Away to the right is Dittisham Mill Creek; beyond it, a part of Higher Dittisham can be spied. It is not until we pass around the next enormous bend that Lower Dittisham looms into view.

We are now in the broadest reach of the river, which is more like a lake. The sweep taken by the ferries is way out on the eastern margin, where the deeper water lies. To the left, Waddeton Court is set well back, as is the hamlet of the same name. And so too is the large village of Galmpton, one of the two places in the county so named. (The other is on the narrow road leading down to Hope Cove, in the corner of Bigbury Bay.)

The County Directory for 1914 lists its entry under that of neighbouring Churston Ferrers, which had the benefit of the parish church: *GALMPTON, hamlet... nearly the whole of the cottages have been rebuilt and a number of houses erected within the last few years. The Flavell Congregational chapel was erected in 1870 at a cost of £400.* There wasn't a lot more to say about it, other than that the Manor Inn was trading then and Sanders & Co were ship builders.

Galmpton was home to Kenneth Wolstenholme (1920–2002), the popular soccer commentator who gave us that memorable quote, "Some people are on the pitch... they think it's all over... It is now!"

Down the Dart

During the Second World War, Kenneth was a twice-decorated bomber pilot, with both the Distinguished Flying Cross and the Bar to the DFC. He was the first presenter of *Match of the Day* in 1964. In his later years, he worked on Italian football programmes shown on Channel Four, and his distinctive, easy-on-the-ear voice was often used for television commercials.

Galmpton's disused sandstone quarries, closer to the river, were the source of the stone used for Totnes's impressive parish church tower, which appeared earlier in the book.

Having negotiated this big bend in the river, the boat now heads on in the general direction of Dittisham (pronounced 'Ditsum' by many). The Domesday survey of 1085-86 lists it as 'Didashim', meaning the homestead of Deedas.

The village is famous for its plum orchards, which still exist, albeit on a much smaller scale than in past times. The delicious 'Plowman' variety (similar to the 'Victoria') is believed to be unique to Dittisham; the liqueur made from it is said to be delicious.

Bill Giles, the television weatherman who retired in 2000, was born here in 1939. It was also probably the birthplace of Francis Rous in 1579. Educated at Oxford and the University of Leyden, he became a Member of Parliament for Truro (1625–1656). He is best remembered for the popular hymn 'The Lord's My Shepherd', which is based on Psalm 23.

From the top of the village, the parish church of St George overlooks the river. There are many features of interest in this ancient place of worship, among them a grand stone pulpit, in a wineglass shape, which glistens like gold.

We are now in the heart of 'Christie country'. Dame Agatha was born at 'Ashfield' in Barton Road, Torquay, on 15 September 1890 and christened Agatha Mary Clarissa Miller. Her father was an American businessman; her mother was English. During the First World War she worked in a Torquay dispensary, where she gained invaluable knowledge of poisons and chemicals.

She married Colonel Archibald Christie on Christmas Eve 1914, after he had proposed at the Pavilion in Torquay (now a shopping complex). They had a daughter in 1919, but things didn't work out and they divorced in 1926.

Four years later she married Sir Max Mallowan. In 1938, having enjoyed immense success as a writer, she bought Greenway House, shown above but now hidden by trees, on the hill above the river. Having achieved both fame and fortune, Dame Agatha Christie passed away at the age of 85 in January 1976, in Oxfordshire, where she had another home.

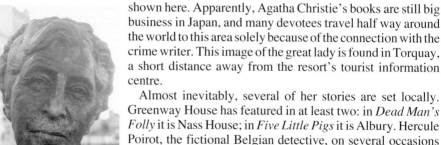

At the end of 1999 her daughter, Rosalind Hicks, gifted the superb garden at Greenway to the National Trust. Although the gardens can be visited, Greenway House is not open to the public.

A specially designed trail has been established at Torquay so that Christie fans can find the places that she regularly visited; the symbols that lead from place to place are like the one

shown here. Apparently, Agatha Christie's books are still big business in Japan, and many devotees travel half way around the world to this area solely because of the connection with the crime writer. This image of the great lady is found in Torquay, a short distance away from the resort's tourist information centre.

Almost inevitably, several of her stories are set locally. Greenway House has featured in at least two: in *Dead Man's Folly* it is Nass House; in *Five Little Pigs* it is Albury. Hercule Poirot, the fictional Belgian detective, on several occasions travelled on the steam railway, which runs close to the house. Galmpton village features in *Dead Man's Folly* under the name of Nassecombe, and Maypool Youth Hostel (shown on page 21) became Hoodown Youth Hostel in the same story.

Many of her books have been adapted for television or films and several, like *Ordeal By Innocence*, starring Donald Sutherland, were filmed in South Devon.

Greenway House has other famous connections. Built in about 1780, there are ruins of an earlier Tudor house nearby. This was the birthplace of Humphrey Gilbert, the half-brother of Sir Walter Raleigh. Their mother was Katherine Champernowne of Modbury, who married Walter Raleigh senior after the death of her first husband Otho Gilbert. Sir Humphrey (c.1539–1583) was an English scholar and soldier who became famous as a

navigator and explorer. He supposed that there was a North-West Passage by water across the North American continent that would lead directly to the East Indies. He also devised daring and far-reaching projects for overseas colonisation. Although brilliant and creative, his poor leadership was blamed for his failure to establish the first permanent English colony in North America. He succeeded, however, in annexing Newfoundland.

Down the Dart

The boathouse by the river's edge is claimed to have belonged to Sir Walter Raleigh.

How much you will see of the Anchor Stone, to the right of mid-stream a short way below Greenway, will depend upon the state of the tide: the lower the water, the more you will see. It is marked by a red pole with a red can attached to its top so that boats do not run into it. The legends about it vary with the tell-ing. Some refer to Sir Walter Raleigh sitting on it at low water, blissfully smoking a pipe. Others, aware of its alternative name of the 'Scold Stone', have it as a point of punish-ment for unfaithful or waspish wives, whose husbands dumped them there to reflect on their short-comings. It was felt an exile on the rock would persuade them to be-come more loyal or civil.

Just to the east of Greenway, Maypool is briefly glimpsed from the river. It was designed by Robert Medley Fulford, a talented architect. Today it is a youth hostel. It was built for F. C. Simpson (of Simpson, Strickland & Co Ltd), who ran a boat-building yard (now the site of Philip & Son Ltd and the Noss-on-Dart Marina) which we will soon pass.

Apparently the house has an abundance of woodwork because the nearby shipyard had accrued a considerable surplus of timber. As new vessels were rarely being built in wood at the time (1880s), it seemed prudent to 'recycle' the timber.

Simpson's firm, a rival to Philip & Son, specialised in building steam sailing yachts for rich clients. It thrived until the First World War but, unlike its neighbours, did not diversify enough to ride out the business consequences of the conflict. Nevertheless, it is still possible to see evidence of its output: the excellent Brixham Museum holds many drawings of Simpson-Strickland craft. Various boat owners all around the country still proudly possess items of working equipment from this firm.

A pilgrimage half way around the world would be necessary to see one former vessel from this yard. The fate of the *Ohura*, a 50-ton, 86-foot-long vessel, was sealed on 6 May 1940 when she tragically overturned on the treacherous Ngaporo Rapid on the Wanganui River in New Zealand. Her cargo of cattle and sheep had panicked and they all shifted to one side of the boat. This imbalance caused the boat to capsize, the sheep following the cattle into the turbulent waters. Three men lost their lives. After being salvaged, the *Ohura* was withdrawn from service and given to B. Bullock & Co of Wanganui to be used as a barge. In the 1950s she sank in mud, where her hulk rests to this day.

Mr Simpson's firm had some talented employees. Within the ranks was Albert Liwentaal, a Swiss-born engineer who took a keen interest in studying the flight of local sea birds. This brush with nature inspired him to design a revolutionary flying machine. A sympathetic local boat-builder kindly allowed him to assemble it in his very large shed. When ready, it was conveyed by boat up river to Gurrow Point. With great difficulty, his team of voluntary helpers managed to carry it up the hill above Dittisham Mill Creek, a place we passed earlier. Thus, in the spring of 1894, perched high on a bicycle saddle, this brave young man was intent on becoming airborne 'aboard' his *Dittisham Aerostat*, a would-be flying machine with a 40-foot wing span.

Picture the scene then as his friends, endeavouring to balance the wing tips, ran down the steep slope beside him. The 'flight' (for want of a better term) was a hit and miss affair. He managed to get about six feet off the ground for a brief time, but a sudden gust of wind

Down the Dart

flipped the machine over. Considerable damage was sustained to the craft, but Albert, bruised and battered, was determined to succeed. He effected repairs, to himself and to his machine, and made another bold attempt at nearby Bozomzeal. This time he was less successful. He not only failed to get off the ground, but crashed heavily into an unyielding hedgerow. His machine was a write-off and poor Albert, his wings truly clipped, was carted off to Dartmouth hospital, much the worse for wear for his 'aerial' antics. When he recovered from the accident, he moved to London and out of the local limelight.

It was nearly ten years later, in 1903, that the first successful, sustained powered flights in a heavier-than-air machine were made by Wilbur and Orville Wright at Kill Devil Hill. Dedicated in 1932, a 60-foot granite monument was placed on the hill in North Carolina to commemorate the achievement of these two pioneer aviators. And to think it could have been here instead: a landmark that never was!

The jungle-like woods create an impressive backcloth to the river. Indeed, the producers of one of the series of the BBC's *The Onedin Line* used them as a cheap substitute for the Amazon rainforest. Rubber alligators moored to rafts worked well, but the overall deception had its drawbacks. In one episode, clouds of smoke billowed above the Amazon forest canopy. But this was not the indigenous population of Amazonian Indians sending smoke signals; it was the steam train heading towards Churston! (See overleaf.)

The river straightens out below Greenway, as Dartmouth and Kingswear come into view. The Philip & Son shipyard was founded in 1858 by George Philip, a canny Scot who had settled in Dartmouth four years earlier. He became a foreman shipwright with Mr Kelly, who rented a small boatyard at Sandquay. On Kelly's retirement, the ambitious Philip took over.

He took his son Alexander (Alec) into the firm shortly afterwards. They built fishing vessels, wooden schooners, launches and yachts. George Philip died in 1874, and the yard passed first to his son then, on his death, to his two grandsons.

Down the Dart

During the First World War the yard undertook naval and government work. Expansion was impossible at Sandquay so, in partnership with Swan Hunter, the firm purchased the Noss Shipyard on the opposite bank of the river. In bankrolling this bold venture, the controlling interest became the privilege of the parent company.

In 1935 the successful construction of a lightship for Trinity House led to seven more being built over the next four years. The Second World War disrupted trade and another shift in emphasis followed. Almost 200 craft of various types were built, including minelayers, minesweepers, corvettes, and a veritable fleet of smaller craft.

Tragedy struck during an air raid on 18 September 1942: twenty of the workforce were killed and many more injured.

Following the war, things began to get back to normal. In September 1952 the Commissioners of Irish Lights ordered the first of several lightvessels from this yard; named *Gannet,* she was launched on 6 May 1954.

The general depression which hit British shipbuilding in the 1960s was also unkind to the boatyard. The company adapted and diversified as best it could to stay 'afloat', but ultimately failed. Orders for private yachts were insufficient to keep the yard fully manned and redundancies followed.

But it wasn't all doom and gloom; the marina was developed and the famous yacht *British Steel* was constructed over the following two years. Chay Blyth, the world-famous yachtsman, sailed it single-handed around the world. The yard also built a trawler in 1995 and completed two steel fishing vessels in 1999. However, in October that year the company decided to discontinue ship and boat building because of the state of the fishing industry. It is inevitable that the environs of the Noss boatyard will witness further massive change.

Disappearing to a visible tapering point, the long inlet on the right-hand side is Old Mill Creek. On the hill above is the Britannia Royal Naval College, which comes into view on the starboard side in a short while. On the water, naval cadets will probably be seen learning new skills in smaller craft (whalers or picket boats) than they will encounter in their post-Dartmouth careers.

The beginning of this famous institution dates back to 30 September 1863. It was then that the wooden warship HMS *Britannia* arrived on the River Dart to be moored off Sandquay. In those formative times, young cadets arrived at the age of 13 to undergo five years of training, involving academic study and seamanship. Its success was such that more accommodation was soon required. To fill the need, another old warship, HMS *Hindustan* (or *Hindostan*), was introduced. The demand continued to pose problems; within four years the *Britannia* gave way to the more spacious *Prince of Wales*. For the sake of continuity, she was renamed *Britannia*.

Well, nothing succeeds like success. In the 1890s the Navy eyed the possibility of a shore-based college, and the nearby hillside looked to be an inviting site. The land having been acquired (by compulsory purchase), the foundation stone was laid by Edward VII on 7 March 1902. Designed by Sir Aston Webb (1849–1930), the college was completed and opened three and a half years later, on 14 September 1905. It looks most impressive when viewed from the Kingswear side of the river, or from the air.

Down the Dart

One of the favourite anecdotes regarding this establishment is that this is where, in 1939, the 13-year-old Princess Elizabeth first set eyes on her future husband.

Prince Philip of Greece and Denmark was born on Corfu on 10 June 1921, to Prince Andrew of Greece and Princess Alice, the eldest daughter of Louis Alexander Mountbatten. He inherited his titles from his father, who was a grandson of the Danish monarch Christian IX. He spent the first years of his life in France, before attending Cheam Preparatory School. From here, he graduated to Gordonstoun, before moving on to the Royal Naval College at Dartmouth. Later, the young man rose quickly through the ranks to become second in command of the Fleet destroyer HMS *Whelp*.

In January 1946, he began to court the young Princess Elizabeth, one of his distant cousins. Their engagement was announced 18 months later; by then he was a British

subject, having renounced his right to the Greek and Danish thrones. He had also adopted his mother's maiden name of Mountbatten.

Throughout the years, royalty has had much to do with the college. Incidentally, although you hopefully won't see it, the muddy bed of the Dart is owned by the Duchy of Cornwall.

The river journey is almost done. The floating bridge of the Higher Ferry is passed, and the long embankment runs almost parallel with our course into Dartmouth.

What a town this is, with people thronging a broad waterfront overlooked by a variety of unusual and attractive buildings. Behind the lower part of the town centre, hills as steep as cliffs rise up several hundred feet, with the buildings which populate the lower slopes peering over one another to gain views of the Dart.

Steeped in history, there's much more to Dartmouth than meets the eye! Even where we land there is something of unique interest. The trivia questions asks: where was the only station in England that had no railway lines, but you could buy a railway ticket?

When you get off at the pontoon you will see the answer in a building which resembles a station, but is now an aptly-named restaurant. This was where you could purchase rail tickets and then sit in a typical railway waiting room – but the train journey didn't begin until the passenger ferry had taken you across to the station at Kingswear.

Down the Dart

Many hundreds of thousands of visitors have travelled this way before you, and the scenery is such that it has made its mark on most of them. A century ago, the Revd Sabine Baring Gould, who wrote the words of 'Onward Christian Soldiers', travelled down the river. He had been thwarted in his attempts to take an extended continental holiday, so decided instead to take a short break and visit Dartmouth for the first time: *The descent of the Dart should be made as I made it then, on an early summer evening when the sun is in decline, and the lawns are yellow with buttercups, when the mighty oaks and beeches are casting long shadows, and the reaches of the river are alternately sheets of quivering gold and purple ink.*

As I went down the river, all dissatisfaction at my lot passed away, and by the time Dartmouth came in view I could no longer refrain myself, but threw my cap in the air, and barely caught it from falling overboard as I shouted, "Hurrah for merry England!" Verily it has scenes that are unrivalled in the whole world.

Should you get that feeling of déjà-vu on reaching Dartmouth, when you know that you have never been there before, it can be explained. Almost everything about the place is

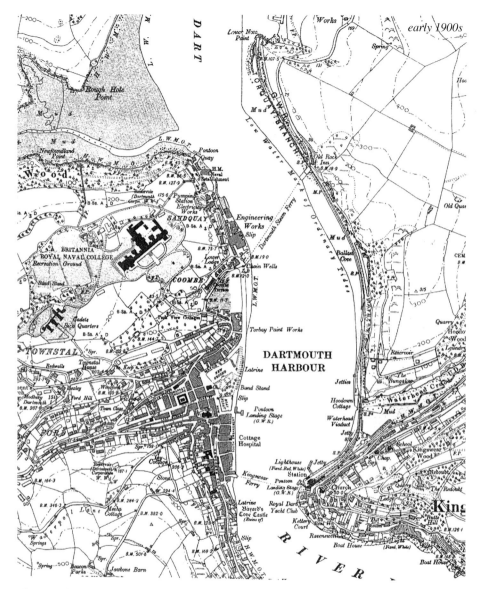

photogenic. This has been recognised by television-programme and film makers; it was Liverpool in *The Onedin Line*, Aberdeen in *The Master of Ballantrae* and a variety of unnamed locations for many more productions. Among the many stars to have filmed here are Emma Thompson, Kris Kristofferson, Michael Elphick, Christian Slater, Twiggy, Meryl Streep, Donald Sutherland, Jeremy Irons, Oliver Tobias and Anthony Hopkins. More recently, Ricky Tomlinson was a colourful and larger-than-life sight around town when scenes for the BBC television series *Down to Earth* were filmed here.

Having stepped from the boat onto the pontoon, you are just about back on terra firma – 'just about' as most of the flat land in the town is reclaimed from the estuary.

Down the Dart

If you can, take some time out to go back to explore the many other places along the way or, if you wish to do this from the comfort of your easy chair, you can acquire some of the many books we have published about the South Hams area. Either way, you won't regret the investment of time or money. The Revd Sabine Baring-Gould was spot on: *Verily it has scenes that are unrivalled in the whole world.*

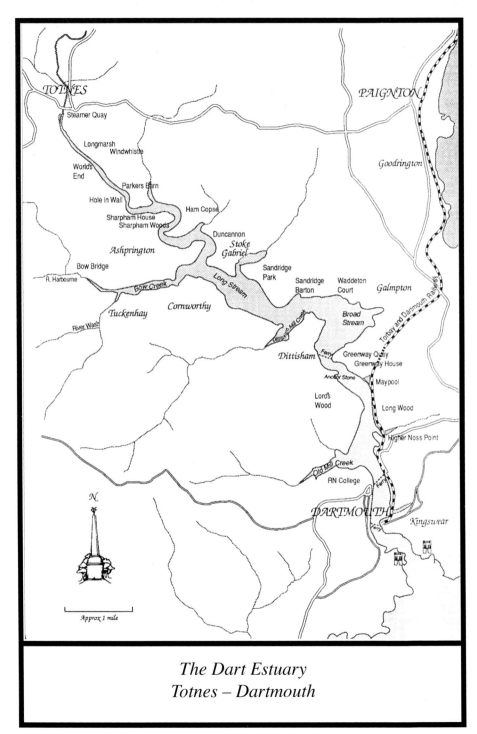

The Dart Estuary
Totnes – Dartmouth